# LAND and WATER
# Lake Erie

by Anne Ylvisaker

**Consultant:**
Rosanne W. Fortner, Professor of Natural Resources
and Associate Director, F. T. Stone Laboratory
The Ohio State University
School of Natural Resources
Columbus, Ohio

Capstone
press

Mankato, Minnesota

Fact Finders is published by Capstone Press
151 Good Counsel Drive, P.O. Box 669, Mankato, Minnesota 56002
http://www.capstone-press.com

*Library of Congress Cataloging-in-Publication Data*
Ylvisaker, Anne.
    Lake Erie / by Anne Ylvisaker.
    v. cm.—(Fact finders. Land and water)
    Includes bibliographical references and index.
    Contents: Lake Erie—Lake Beginnings—Lake Erie's people—Water highways—
Pollution—Lake Erie today—Hands on activity.
    ISBN 0-7368-2208-9
    1. Erie, Lake—Juvenile literature. [1. Erie, Lake.] I. Title. II. Series.
F555.Y58 2004
977.1'2—dc21                                                      2002156575

**Editorial Credits**
Erika L. Shores, editor; Juliette Peters, designer; Alta Schaffer, photo researcher;
    Eric Kudalis, product planning editor

**Photo Credits**
Cover image: Point Abino Lighthouse on Lake Erie, James P. Rowan

Corbis/Bettmann, 12–13; Charles Rotkin, 20–21
C. W. Jefferys/National Archives of Canada, 14
The Image Finders/Jim Baron, 1, 10, 11, 16–17, 22–23, 24–25, 26–27
James Blank/Root Resources, 15
Library of Congress, 4–5
North Wind Picture Archives, 18, 19

The Hands On activity on page 29 was adapted with permission from "How Big Is a
Crowd?" by R. W. Fortner and D. Jax, LAKERS Observe Coastweeks, Sea Grant Education
Program, Columbus, Ohio.

1 2 3 4 5 6 08 07 06 05 04 03

# Table of Contents

# Chapter 1

# Lake Erie

"Don't give up the ship!" A blue flag with these words flew from the *Lawrence*, a ship led by U.S. Lieutenant Oliver Perry. The United States was fighting Great Britain in the War of 1812 (1812–1814). Both countries wanted control of the Great Lakes. Perry led U.S. soldiers during the Battle of Lake Erie at Put-in-Bay.

As Perry's ship sailed forward, British ships fired cannons. The *Lawrence* was badly damaged. Most of its sailors were hurt or killed. Perry did not give up. He jumped into a rowboat. British soldiers shot at the rowboat as it neared the *Niagara*, another U.S. ship.

Oliver Perry led the Battle of Lake Erie at Put-in-Bay.

Aboard the *Niagara*, Perry continued to lead the fight. Finally, two British ships crashed into each other. The British gave up. The United States won control of Lake Erie and its nearby territory.

# The Great Lakes

Lakes Superior, Huron, Michigan, Ontario, and Erie are the Great Lakes of North America. Rivers and canals connect all five of the Great Lakes like water highways. Ships can travel from the Atlantic Ocean to the middle of North America on these water highways.

Like most Great Lakes, Lake Erie lies between the United States and Canada. The U.S. state of Michigan borders the lake to the west. The province of Ontario, Canada, lies to the north. New York, Pennsylvania, and Ohio border Lake Erie to the south and east.

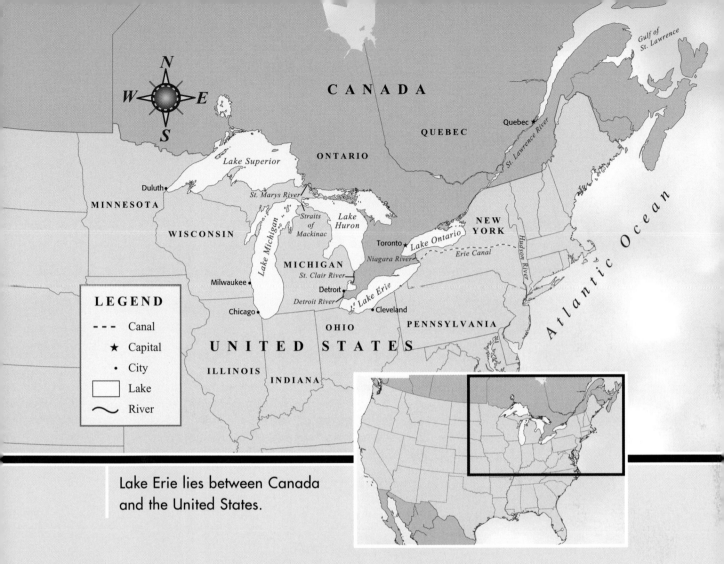

LEGEND

--- Canal
★ Capital
• City
□ Lake
~ River

Lake Erie lies between Canada and the United States.

Lake Erie is the 11th largest lake in the world. It is 241 miles (388 kilometers) long and 57 miles (92 kilometers) wide. Lake Erie is the shallowest of the Great Lakes. Its average depth is only 62 feet (19 meters).

# Chapter 2

# Lake Beginnings

Thousands of years ago, glaciers covered the Great Lakes area. These slow-moving sheets of ice were more than 1 mile (2 kilometers) thick. The glaciers' weight pressed the land down. They moved rocks that scraped the earth. Together, the pressure and scraping carved wide valleys. When the glaciers melted, water filled the valleys. The Great Lakes were formed.

Lake Erie is shallow and much of it is surrounded by flat land. Wetlands cover some of Lake Erie's shore. More than 300 kinds of wildflowers and 300 kinds of birds live there.

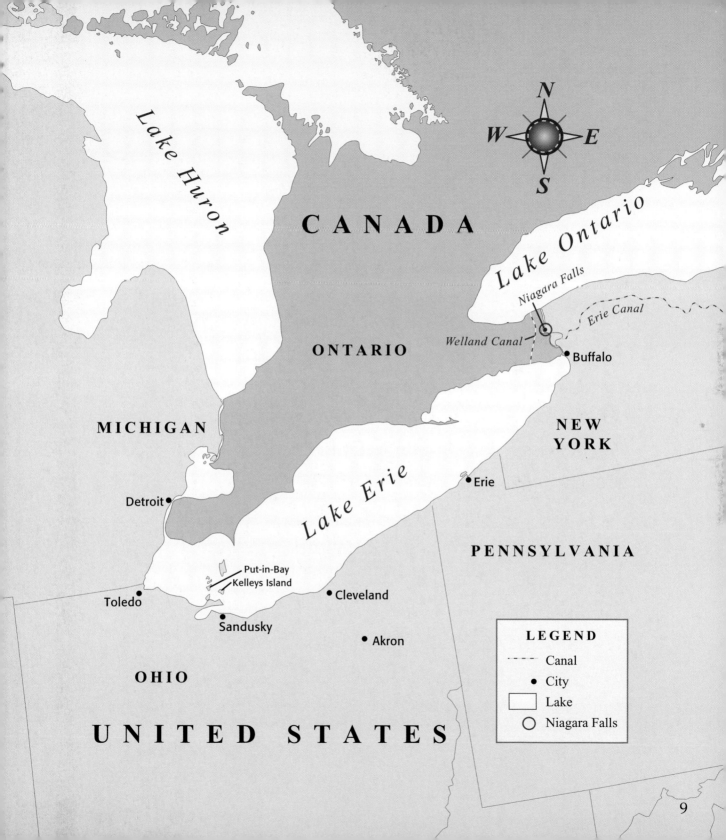

Lake Huron

CANADA

N
W ● E
S

Lake Ontario

Niagara Falls

Erie Canal

ONTARIO

Welland Canal

● Buffalo

MICHIGAN

NEW
YORK

● Erie

Detroit ●

Lake Erie

PENNSYLVANIA

Put-in-Bay
Kelleys Island

● Cleveland

Toledo ●

● Sandusky

● Akron

OHIO

LEGEND
- - - Canal
● City
☐ Lake
◎ Niagara Falls

UNITED STATES

9

Large waves can crash onto Lake Erie's shores.

## Dangerous Waves

Storms can be strong on Lake Erie. Most storms come in from the west. They move across the lake and push the water eastward. Water piles up at the eastern shore. The water then sloshes back like water in a bathtub. The sloshing motion is called a seiche (SAYSH). At the east end, the high water does little damage. The shore is high and rocky. At the west end, the land is low and flat. High water from storms may flood farms and towns.

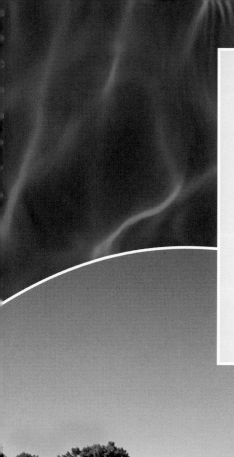

## Kelleys Island

Kelleys Island is a National Historic Landmark near Sandusky, Ohio. People bike or ride in golf carts to get around the island.

Visitors to the island can see many sites. Glacial Grooves State Memorial is on Kelleys Island. Visitors can see the grooves that glaciers left in the rocks. At Inscription Rock State Memorial, visitors can see carvings left by Erie

# Chapter 3

# Lake Erie's People

Native people of North America lived near Lake Erie for thousands of years. They grew corn and beans in the rich soil around the lake. They fished in the lake. They also hunted in the nearby forests. Lake Erie is named for the Erie Indians who lived on the south shores of the lake. The Neutral Indians lived north of Lake Erie. Over time, the Iroquois Indians forced the Erie and Neutral Indians out of the area.

In the 1600s, the Iroquois Indians protected their land around Lake Erie from early European explorers. The Iroquois fought many battles with Europeans who hoped to settle the land around the lake.

French explorers, with the help of other American Indian groups, often fought with the Iroquois.

## Explorers

Lake Erie was the last Great Lake to be explored by Europeans. In the 1600s, French explorers came to the area from Canada. They were looking for a water route to China. They also wanted to

trade with the native people in the area.

French explorer Étienne Brulé may have visited Lake Erie as early as 1615. French explorer Louis Jolliett came in 1669.

Priests often traveled with explorers. The priests kept written records of the journeys. They wrote about what they saw and the people they met. Father Louis Hennepin came to Lake Erie. He drew pictures to go with the writings of what he saw. Hennepin was the first European to see Niagara Falls.

Étienne Brulé explored Lake Erie.

## Niagara Falls

Niagara is an Indian word meaning "Thunder of the Waters." Water pours over a limestone ledge 326 feet (99 meters) above the Niagara River. Thousands of people visit Niagara Falls each year. Visitors can ride boats out to see the falls and feel the powerful spray.

# Chapter 4

# Water Highways

Water travel between the Great Lakes and the Atlantic Ocean was not always possible. Rapids and waterfalls along the rivers were dangerous to ships. Water was too shallow for ships in some areas. People dug canals so ships could travel between the lakes. They added locks that could raise and lower ships to different water levels.

The Erie Canal joins Lake Erie to the Atlantic Ocean. Work began on the canal in 1817. It took eight years to finish. Ships can travel 363 miles (584 kilometers) from Lake Erie to the Hudson River on the canal. The Hudson River then empties into the Atlantic Ocean.

Ships enter Cleveland's
Cuyahoga River from Lake Erie.

Other canals were later built to join Lake Erie to rivers in nearby states. Ships traveled on the canals to bring goods to people living in Ohio, Pennsylvania, and New York.

Locks were built to help boats travel between the lakes.

Shipping on the Great Lakes helped cities such as Buffalo, New York, grow.

Limestone, iron ore, and coal were brought to cities from Lake Superior. Workers came from around the world to make iron ore into steel. Steel was used to make ships. Later, cars and airplanes were made with steel.

# Chapter 5

# Pollution

In the 1960s, people saw that Lake Erie was in trouble. Slimy plants called algae grew on the water. Few fish lived in the lake.

Two factors combined to damage Lake Erie. Chemicals for fertilizing lawns and crops washed into the lake. These chemicals caused algae to grow. Factories dumped waste into the water. Algae soaked up the chemicals in the waste.

Lake Erie's algae caused problems for the environment. Small animals and fish ate the algae. A few of these creatures died. The creatures who lived

Laws were passed in the 1970s to protect Lake Erie from pollution.

had chemicals in their bodies. Some were no longer able to reproduce young.

Many fish had to leave Lake Erie. Fish breathe oxygen in the water through their gills. But there was not enough oxygen in some areas of Lake

Erie. Bacteria used up the oxygen as the algae began to die. The fish moved to the other Great Lakes.

In 1972, Canada and the United States began the International Great Lakes Water Quality Agreement. New laws stopped factories from dumping waste into the lake. Farmers found ways to use less fertilizer. Cities along the lake cleaned up waste that would wash into the lake. These efforts helped clean the lake's water and beaches.

Today, Lake Erie is cleaner. Healthy fish swim in the lake. People enjoy fishing and visiting the beaches along Lake Erie.

Lake Erie's beaches are popular tourist spots.

# Chapter 6

# Lake Erie Today

Industry and transportation helped many cities around Lake Erie to grow. Today, steel mills, natural gas wells, and glass factories surround the lake. Akron, Ohio, is the rubber capital of the world. Tires for cars and trucks are made in Akron's factories.

The climate and rich soil near Lake Erie are good for growing crops. Concord grapes for fruit juices are harvested between Buffalo, New York, and Erie, Pennsylvania.

Cleveland, Ohio, is a large city on Lake Erie.

Many people enjoy the lake. Sailing and boating are popular sports on Lake Erie. Marinas line the lakeshore. People rent docks for their boats and dine at the marinas. Other people hike along miles of

nature trails around the lake. Hikers look at the many kinds of birds and wildflowers. People who live and work near Lake Erie are pleased that the lake is healthy again. They continue to work to keep it clean.

Boats dock at marinas on Lake Erie's shores.

# *Fast Facts*

**Length:** 241 miles (388 kilometers)

**Width:** 57 miles (92 kilometers)

**Average depth:** 62 feet (19 meters)

**Maximum depth:** 210 feet (64 meters)

**Shoreline length:** 871 miles (1,402 kilometers)

**Population surrounding the lake:** 12.4 million

**Name:** The word Erie means "cat" in the Erie Indian language. It was probably first used to describe the panthers that lived near the lake.

**Weather:** Lake Erie's water warms quickly in spring and summer. Areas of the lake freeze over quickly in winter.

**Fish:** Many kinds of fish live in Lake Erie. Common fish are yellow perch, walleye, smallmouth bass, carp, lake sturgeon, and freshwater drum.

# *Hands On:* A Problem with People

Before the 1970s, people living near the Great Lakes often let trash and waste get into the lakes. Lakes that had a lot of people living near them became polluted. Today, people work to keep the lakes clean. Play this game to see how the number of people living near a lake affects it.

## What You Need

Paved outdoor area
  protected from wind
Chalk
Group of friends

Five bags of peanuts in their shells or
  sunflower seeds in their shells
Timekeeper

## What You Do

1. Draw three chalk circles next to one another. Each circle should be about 4 feet (1.2 meters) across. Label these circles from left to right: Lake Superior, Lake Michigan, Lake Huron.
2. Draw two circles that are 2 feet (.6 meter) across to the bottom and left of the Lake Huron circle. Label the last two circles from left to right: Lake Erie and Lake Ontario.
3. Assign players to stand in the circles as follows: Lake Superior—no one; Lake Michigan—four players; Lake Huron—one player; Lake Erie—three players; Lake Ontario—two players.
6. The timekeeper gives one person in each circle a bag of peanuts or sunflower seeds to hold. The timekeeper says "Go," and begins keeping time.
7. Players in each circle take a peanut or seed out of the bag. They open their peanuts or seeds, eat them, and pass the bag to the next person in the circle. The person in Lake Huron does not pass his or her bag.
8. Players hurry to pass and eat as many peanuts or seeds as they can.
9. After two minutes, the timekeeper says "Stop."
10. Players now stand outside of the circles. Why might Lake Erie and Lake Ontario have the most shells on the ground?

Try playing the game again. This time think of ways to keep the shells from "polluting" the lakes.

# Glossary

**algae** (AL-jee)—small plants without roots or stems that grow in water or on damp surfaces

**canal** (kuh-NAL)—a channel that is dug across land; canals connect bodies of water so that ships can travel between them.

**glacier** (GLAY-shur)—a large, slow-moving sheet of ice and snow

**industry** (IN-duh-stree)—businesses that make products or provide services

**lock** (LOK)—an area of water with gates at both ends; locks help ships move from one water level to another.

**marina** (muh-REE-nuh)—a small harbor where boats are stored

**port** (PORT)—a place where boats and ships can dock or anchor safely

# Internet Sites

Do you want to find out more about Lake Erie?
Let FactHound, our fact-finding hound dog, do the research for you.

Here's how:
1) Visit *http://www.facthound.com*
2) Type in the **BOOK ID** number: **0736822089**
3) Click on **FETCH IT**.

FactHound will fetch Internet sites picked by our editors just for you!

# Read More

**Beckett, Harry.** *Lake Erie.* Great Lakes of North America.
Vero Beach, Fla: Rourke, 1999.

**Englar, Mary.** *The Iroquois: The Six Nations Confederacy.* American
Indian Nations. Mankato, Minn.: Bridgestone Books, 2003.

# Index